P9-CCX-619

Green Eggs and Ham Cookbook

Recipes inspired by

Dr. Seuss!

Concocted by Georgeanne Brennan

and photographed by Frankie Frankeny

RANDOM HOUSE ⌂ NEW YORK

TM & copyright © 2006 by Dr. Seuss Enterprises, L.P.

Text copyright © 2006 by Georgeanne Brennan (excluding Dr. Seuss excerpts)
Photographs copyright © 2006 by Frankie Frankeny (excluding Dr. Seuss images)

All rights reserved.

Published in the United States by Random House Children's Books, a division of Random House, Inc., New York.

RANDOM HOUSE and colophon are registered trademarks of Random House, Inc.

www.randomhouse.com/kids

www.seussville.com

Educators and librarians, for a variety of teaching tools, visit us at www.randomhouse.com/teachers

Excerpted text and art by Dr. Seuss contained in this work were originally published as follows: *If I Ran the Zoo,* TM & copyright © by Dr. Seuss Enterprises, L.P. 1950, renewed 1978. *Yertle the Turtle and Other Stories,* TM & copyright © by Dr. Seuss Enterprises, L.P. 1950, 1951, 1958, renewed 1977, 1979, 1986. *Scrambled Eggs Super!,* TM & copyright © by Dr. Seuss Enterprises, L.P. 1953. *If I Ran the Circus,* TM & copyright © by Dr. Seuss Enterprises, L.P. 1956, renewed 1984. *How the Grinch Stole Christmas!,* TM & copyright © by Dr. Seuss Enterprises, L.P. 1957, renewed 1985. *The Cat in the Hat Comes Back,* TM & copyright © by Dr. Seuss Enterprises, L.P. 1958, renewed 1986. *Happy Birthday to You!,* TM & copyright © by Dr. Seuss Enterprises, L.P. 1959, renewed 1987. *Green Eggs and Ham,* copyright © by Dr. Seuss Enterprises, L.P. 1960, renewed 1988. *One Fish Two Fish Red Fish Blue Fish,* copyright © by Dr. Seuss Enterprises, L.P. 1960, renewed 1988. *The Sneetches and Other Stories,* copyright © by Dr. Seuss Enterprises, L.P. 1953, 1954, 1961, renewed 1989, 2004. *Dr. Seuss's Sleep Book,* TM & copyright © by Dr. Seuss Enterprises, L.P. 1962, renewed 1990. *Dr. Seuss's ABC,* TM & copyright © by Dr. Seuss Enterprises, L.P. 1963, renewed 1991. *Hop on Pop,* copyright © by Dr. Seuss Enterprises, L.P. 1963, renewed 1991. *Fox in Socks,* copyright © by Dr. Seuss Enterprises, L.P. 1965, renewed 1993. *I Had Trouble in Getting to Solla Sollew,* copyright © by Dr. Seuss Enterprises, L.P. 1965, renewed 1993. *The Cat in the Hat Songbook,* TM & copyright © by Dr. Seuss Enterprises, L.P. and Eugene Poddany, 1967. Copyright renewed 1995 by Dr. Seuss Enterprises, L.P. and Oleg Poddany. *I Can Lick 30 Tigers Today! and Other Stories,* copyright © by Dr. Seuss Enterprises, L.P. 1969, renewed 1997. *The Lorax,* ® & copyright © by Dr. Seuss Enterprises, L.P. 1971, renewed 1999. *Did I Ever Tell You How Lucky You Are?,* copyright © 1973 by Dr. Seuss and A. S. Geisel, renewed 2001 by Dr. Seuss Enterprises, L.P. *There's a Wocket in My Pocket!,* TM & copyright © by Dr. Seuss Enterprises, L.P. 1974, renewed 2002. *Oh, the Thinks You Can Think!,* TM & copyright © by Dr. Seuss Enterprises, L.P. 1975, renewed 2003. *The Cat's Quizzer,* TM & copyright © 1976 by 1984 Geisel Trust, renewed 2004 by Dr. Seuss Enterprises, L.P. *I Can Read with My Eyes Shut!,* TM & copyright © by Dr. Seuss Enterprises, L.P. 1978. *Oh Say Can You Say?,* TM & copyright © by Dr. Seuss Enterprises, L.P. 1979. *Daisy-Head Mayzie,* TM & copyright © by Dr. Seuss Enterprises, L.P. 1994.

Library of Congress Cataloging-in-Publication Data
Brennan, Georgeanne, 1943–
Green eggs and ham cookbook / recipes inspired by Dr. Seuss,
concocted by Georgeanne Brennan and photographed by Frankie Frankeny. — 1st ed.
  p. cm.
ISBN-13: 978-0-679-88440-8 — ISBN-10: 0-679-88440-8
1. Cookery—Juvenile literature. I. Frankeny, Frankie, ill. II. Seuss, Dr. Selections. 2006. III. Title.
TX652.5B716 2006   641.5'123—dc22   2005036132

PRINTED IN CHINA 10 9 8 7 6 5 4 3 2 First Edition

Contents

(continued)

Contents (continued)

Dinner

Desserts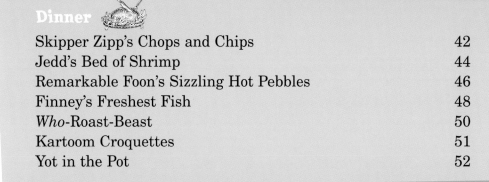

Introduction

I've always wondered what green eggs and ham would *really* taste like and what Dr. Seuss had in mind when he concocted them. Was it spinach? Green food coloring? Surely not basil or pureed broccoli. And just how would you get the yolk green, and what would stick on ham to cover it so neatly and be so bright green? Was it cooked on or added later? Would it really taste good or be just a gimmick? And what exactly was the *Who-roast-beast* and how was it prepared? What in the world were Kartoom Croquettes? And would it really work to combine pickles and eggs in a Scrambled Eggs Super Scramble? (Why not? said my daughter. Pickles with peanut butter are good.) As a passionate cook and a cookbook author, these were the kinds of questions that intrigued me as I read Dr. Seuss's books to my children, and later to myself.

Well, I can tell you that I discovered guacamole works well to cover the fried egg yolk, and that apple jelly glaze added to cooked ham has just the right flavor and stickiness to hold a coating of bright green cilantro. The *Who-Roast-Beast* I devised is made beastly-looking (and tasty) with a bumpity layer of mushrooms tucked under its skin before roasting. And I decided Kartoom Croquettes were best made of chopped chicken, but pickles, I found, were not good in the scramble, although lots of other things were.

Frankie and I perused every single Dr. Seuss book, all 44 of them, and found they were full of wacky foods for us to bring to life, from Yot in the Pot and Fred Food to Truffula Fruits, Ape Cakes Grape Cakes, and Schlopp with a Cherry on Top. Some of the words and images weren't about food at all but were so inspiring they turned into food, like Nupboards in Cupboards (see Nupboards' Nuggets, a granola-like treat) and Schlottz's Knots, which became long, twisted pretzels—what else?

It was important to us that the recipes in the *Green Eggs and Ham Cookbook* be not only Seussian, zany, and fun, but also deliciously good and healthy, too. So you'll find good things like honey, olive oil, yogurt, nuts, grains, cheese, fresh fruits and vegetables, and fish and chicken in the ingredient lists, as well as chocolate, butter, and cream.

I've created the recipes from scratch, so you'll be going from start to finish with fresh ingredients, chopping vegetables to simmer in soup, whisking homemade cheese sauce, pureeing fresh raspberries and kiwis for drinks. You can take shortcuts, too, if you want. Cat in the Hat Tub Cake is made with a purchased angel food cake, and you can buy ready-made doughnuts to decorate for the Brigger-ba-Root Doughnut Shoot.

This is a cookbook for adults and children to use together. A kitchen, as you know, is an exciting, creative place, but there are safety rules to follow, and these are *especially* important when working with children, who tend to get very enthusiastic when cooking.

- Let adults handle sharp knives.
- Let adults turn on the burner and reach into the hot oven.
- Let adults take hot pans from the stovetop.
- Let adults take charge anytime hot oil is being used.
- Let adults operate blenders, food processors, and other electric appliances.

Every recipe has components for children to do—stirring pancake batter, cutting out cookies, rolling fish and croquettes in bread crumbs, painting ham with apple jelly glaze, and assembling s'mores.

Many of the recipes in the book require no chopping, cooking, or electric appliances, so children can do these with just a little supervision. "Fun Is Good" Milk Cow, Silly Sammy Slick's Sodas, Gertrude McFuzz-y Berries, and Schlopp with a Cherry on Top are examples of these.

Most of all, cooking is fun, and everyone benefits from good food, well prepared, by people who care about each other. This is the spirit in which we concocted and photographed the recipes for the *Green Eggs and Ham Cookbook*. This is the spirit in which we both hope you will enjoy making and eating the recipes as much as we enjoyed creating them.

George Brown

Then I mixed in some ginger, nine prunes and three figs
And parsley. Quite sparsely. Just twenty-two sprigs.
Then I added six cinnamon sticks and a clove
And my scramble was ready to go on the stove!

From Scrambled Eggs Super!

Scrambled Eggs Super-Dee-Dooper-Dee-Booper, Special De Luxe à-la-Peter T. Hooper!

Scrambled Eggs Super are super-simple to make, and you can change ingredients or add more, according to whatever *eggs*-cites you—pepperoni or bacon or corned beef hash, green peppers, mushrooms, or broccoli. You decide.

Ingredients

½ tablespoon butter
1½ tablespoons extra-virgin olive oil
8 large eggs, beaten
1 fully cooked sausage, cut into ¼-inch-thick slices
2 tablespoons chopped parsley
2 tablespoons sun-dried tomatoes packed in olive oil, chopped
¼ cup grated cheddar cheese
½ teaspoon salt
¼ teaspoon freshly ground black pepper
½ avocado, peeled, pitted, and cubed

Directions

1. In a large frying pan, melt the butter and olive oil over medium heat.
2. When they are hot, add the eggs, stirring them with a whisk or fork. Reduce the heat to low and add the sausage, parsley, sun-dried tomatoes, cheese, salt, and pepper. Stir until the eggs are no longer runny, about 3 minutes.
3. Add the avocado and gently fold it into the eggs, cooking another 30 seconds.

MAKES 4 TO 5 SERVINGS

Do you like
green eggs and ham? . . .
Would you eat them
in a box?
Would you eat them
with a fox?

From *Green Eggs and Ham*

Green Eggs and Ham

If you, like Sam-I-am, also like green eggs and ham, you will like these green guacamole eggs and green glazed ham—just try them. You can make the guacamole as mild or as spicy as you like. (If you don't want to cook a whole ham, try making a tablespoon or two of the glaze for a slice of ham.) You can eat them here or there. You can eat them anywhere.

Ingredients for Ham

1 fully cooked and smoked ham, about 8 to 10 pounds
1 cup apple or mint apple jelly
3 medium tomatillos, husked and minced
1 cup minced cilantro leaves or ½ cup minced cilantro leaves and ½ cup minced
   parsley leaves

Ingredients for Eggs

4 ripe avocados
juice of 2 to 3 limes
1 teaspoon salt

2 tablespoons white onion, minced (optional)

2 serrano chilies, seeded and minced (optional)

4 ounces butter or 3 tablespoons extra-virgin olive oil or other light cooking oil, such as canola or sunflower

12 pasteurized eggs (pasteurization is necessary for safety when yolks aren't fully cooked)

Directions for Ham

1. Heat the ham as directed by the package instructions. Let cool to almost room temperature, about 20 minutes.

2. Mix the apple jelly and the minced tomatillos together to make a glaze. Spread the ham all over with the glaze, except on the cut side.

3. Using your hands, gently pat the cilantro, or cilantro and parsley, into the glaze until it is solid green.

Directions for Eggs

1. Cut the avocados in half and remove the pits. With a spoon, scoop the flesh out into a bowl. Mash it with a fork, then add the lime juice and salt and, if you want, the onions and chilies. Mix again.

2. In a large frying pan, melt the butter or heat the oil over medium heat. When hot, crack the eggs into the pan.

3. Cover the pan and cook until the yolk has a pale white film over it and is slightly to very firm.

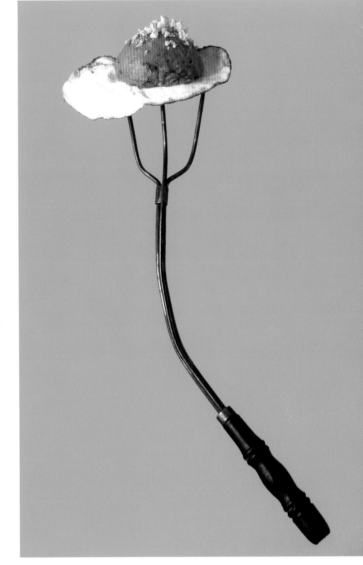

4. With a spatula, gently slide the eggs onto plates or a serving platter.

5. Spoon the guacamole over each yolk, covering it. Serve immediately.

MAKES 12 SERVINGS

Here's a small picture of what the complete recipe looks like. For a larger picture, see the front cover.

And you don't have to stop.
You can think about SCHLOPP.
Schlopp. Schlopp. Beautiful schlopp.
Beautiful schlopp
with a cherry on top.

From *Oh, the Thinks You Can Think!*

Schlopp with a Cherry on Top

Beautiful schlopp is granola, homemade, with honey and orange juice for stick-to-itiveness, seeds, nuts, and oats, and three more good grains of whatever sort you want. Top it all with great glops of yogurt, add some sliced banana, and, of course, plop that cherry on top. You'll want schloppy seconds!

Ingredients for Granola

juice of 1 orange
¼ cup canola, sunflower, or
　　other light cooking oil
¼ cup honey
1 tablespoon sesame seeds
1 tablespoon poppy seeds
1 cup pearled barley
1 cup rolled rye
1 cup quinoa
1 cup oat bran
4 cups uncooked oatmeal
　　(not quick-cooking)
¼ cup chopped walnuts
½ cup golden raisins

Ingredients for Schlopp

1 ripe banana
4 ounces plain or flavored
　　yogurt
1 Maraschino cherry

Directions

1. Preheat the oven to 300°F.
2. In a large bowl, mix together the orange juice, oil, honey, sesame seeds, and poppy seeds.

3. Add the barley, rye, quinoa, oat bran, and rolled oats. Mix until all are well coated, using your hands if necessary.
4. Spread on two large, ungreased baking sheets and bake until lightly toasted, about 45 minutes to 1 hour, stirring every 15 minutes or so. Stir in the walnuts after about 30 minutes.

5. Remove, let cool to room temperature, and stir in the raisins. (May be stored in airtight containers for up to three weeks.)

6. Cut the banana in half and peel it. Cut each half lengthwise to make 4 long slices. If desired, heat in a frying pan or microwave.

7. Put ¼ cup of granola in a bowl, top with half the yogurt, and add the banana slices. Add another ¼ cup of granola and the remaining yogurt and top with the cherry.

MAKES ABOUT 8 CUPS OF GRANOLA AND 1 SERVING OF SCHLOPP

*"I've just called you up to tell you
How I love you. Oh, I do!
And today I did some cooking
And I cooked some Glunker Stew.
Let me tell you how I did it.
You may want to make some, too."*
From "The Glunk That Got Thunk" in *I Can Lick 30 Tigers Today! and Other Stories*

Glunker Stew

The Glunk put berries, straw, lemonade, chicklets, oysters, applesauce, and some more stuff into his stew, and he beat it to a frazzle and spuggled it. This version leaves out the straw, chicklets, and oysters and concentrates on the fruit. Serve with Blueberry Bumplings (page 13).

Ingredients

2 tart apples, such as Granny Smith
2 tablespoons water
1 tablespoon fresh lemon juice
¼ teaspoon cinnamon
1 tablespoon sugar
1 cup fresh or frozen blueberries, thawed
1 cup fresh or frozen raspberries, thawed
¼ cup dried cherries, coarsely chopped

Directions

1. Coarsely chop the apples.
2. Put them in a saucepan with the water, lemon juice, cinnamon, and sugar.
3. Place the pan over low heat. Cook until the apples are soft but still chunky, about 8 to 10 minutes, stirring a few times. Remove from the heat and spoon into a bowl.
4. Gently mix the blueberries and raspberries together in a bowl.
5. Spoon the mixed berries into 4 cereal bowls.
6. Top with a spoonful of the applesauce.
7. Sprinkle with the dried cherries and serve.
MAKES 4 SERVINGS

Donuts, dumplings, blueberry bumplings,
chocolate mush-mush, super sweet.
Clam stew, ham stew, watermelon wush wush,
Oh, the stuff that I could eat!
From *The Cat in the Hat Songbook*

Blueberry Bumplings

The Cat's bumplings are plump things surprisingly like blueberry scones, just right for breakfast or snacking.

Ingredients

2¼ cups all-purpose flour

⅓ cup sugar

2 teaspoons baking powder

¼ teaspoon salt

4 ounces butter, softened and cut into small pieces

½ cup fresh blueberries (½ cup frozen may be substituted)

1 large egg

¾ cup half-and-half

Directions

1. Preheat the oven to 400°F. In a large bowl, combine the flour, sugar, baking powder, and salt.

2. Add the butter and mix well with your fingertips until crumbly, then add the fresh blueberries. (If frozen, add them after step 3.)

3. In a small bowl, mix together the egg and the half-and-half, then quickly beat into the flour mixture. Do not overwork.

4. Pat the dough out between sheets of wax paper or plastic wrap until about ½ inch thick. Cut into 2-inch circles, squares, or triangles.

5. Place the cutouts on a baking sheet, non-stick or lined with parchment paper, and bake until golden on top, about 10 minutes. Serve hot.

MAKES ABOUT 12 BUMPLINGS

 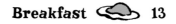

*OR . . . if you think
you don't like cops' caps,
flapjack flappers'
or cupcake cooks' caps,
maybe you're one
of those choosy chaps
who likes kooky captains' caps
perhaps.*

From *Oh Say Can You Say?*

Flapjack Flapper's Flapjacks

Wear a kooky captain's cap instead of a flapjack flapper's cap to flip flapjacks filled with bananas and peanut butter—or flip these flapjacks completely capless!

Ingredients

1 cup all-purpose flour
2 teaspoons baking powder
½ teaspoon salt
2 tablespoons sugar
1 egg
2½ tablespoons creamy or chunky peanut butter
1 cup whole milk
3 tablespoons melted butter plus 1 extra teaspoon
2 bananas, sliced ¼ inch thick
⅓ cup shelled peanuts, salted or unsalted (optional)

Directions

1. In a bowl, combine the flour, baking powder, salt, and sugar and mix well with a whisk.
2. In a large bowl, combine the egg, peanut butter, and milk and beat with an electric mixer.
3. Add the 3 tablespoons of melted butter, then add the flour mixture all at once and beat until extremely smooth, about 2 to 3 minutes. Stir in one-fourth of the banana slices.
4. Grease a griddle or a frying pan with the remaining 1 teaspoon of butter and heat over medium heat.

5. Using a ladle or a measuring cup, pour about ¼ cup of batter for each flapjack, leaving about 2 inches between them. When the top surface is bubbling, the edges opaque, and the bottom side golden brown, after about 1½ minutes, use a spatula to flip each flapjack. Cook until the other side is golden brown, about 45 seconds to 1 minute. Repeat until all the batter is used.
6. Serve stacks of flapjacks with bananas, peanuts, and syrup or honey.
MAKES 10 TO 12 FLAPJACKS

*Did you ever milk
this kind of cow?
Well, we can do it.
We know how.
If you never did,
you should.
These things are fun
and fun is good.*
From *One Fish Two Fish Red Fish Blue Fish*

"Fun *Is* Good" Milk Cow

This kind of cow doesn't moo—can you? It's an ice cream drink that's easy to make, no matter how little you are. You can use any soda you like, from chocolate to cherry to root beer or orange—or all of the above!

Ingredients

1 large scoop of vanilla ice cream (or any kind you want)
8-ounce can or bottle of chocolate soda (or any other kind)
squirt of whipped cream (optional)
1 Maraschino cherry (optional)

Directions

1. Put the scoop of ice cream in a large glass.
2. Pour the soda over it and stir.
3. Top with a squirt of whipped cream and put the cherry on top, if you want to.

MAKES 1 SERVING

A moose is asleep.
He is dreaming of moose drinks.
A goose is asleep.
He is dreaming of goose drinks.
That's well and good when a moose dreams of moose juice.
And nothing goes wrong when a goose dreams of goose juice.
But it isn't too good when a moose and a goose
Start dreaming they're drinking the other one's juice.

From *Dr. Seuss's Sleep Book*

Moose Juice and Goose Juice

Orange is the color of dreamy moose juice, green the color of sleepy goose juice. Orange is made with orange juice, green with kiwi fruit. No mix-up there. Now let's produce moose and goose juice!

Ingredients for Moose Juice

¾ cup orange juice

½ cup orange sherbet

½ banana, sliced

¼ teaspoon vanilla extract

1 tablespoon whipped cream

Ingredients for Goose Juice

3 kiwis, peeled and sliced

¼ cup lime juice or 1½ tablespoons frozen lime concentrate

½ cup lime sherbet

3 ice cubes

1 tablespoon whipped cream

Directions for Moose Juice

1. Combine the orange juice, sherbet, banana, and vanilla extract in a blender. Puree until smooth.

2. Pour into a glass and top with the whipped cream.

MAKES 1 SERVING

Directions for Goose Juice

1. Put the kiwis, lime juice or concentrate, sherbet, and ice cubes in a blender. Puree until smooth.

2. Pour into a glass and top with the whipped cream.

MAKES 1 SERVING

BIG S
little s
Silly Sammy Slick
sipped six sodas
and got
sick sick sick.

From *Dr. Seuss's ABC*

Silly Sammy Slick's Sodas

You won't get sick on these sodas unless you sip six of them like Silly Sammy Slick did. Use any kind of fruit juice you like—grape, orange, cherry, even mango or kiwi. Have a party and make everybody different kinds of sodas. Sodas can be simple, like these, but you can also make them fancy and even more frothy. Use a bigger glass. Add a scoop of ice cream, say, vanilla, to the grape juice, or strawberry ice cream to kiwi juice, then pour in the soda. Don't stop now. Squirt whipped cream from a can on the top and then put a cherry on the top—or maybe two or three if you like cherries a lot.

Ingredients

8 ounces juice
8 ounces club soda

Directions

1. Pour the juice into a 16-ounce glass.
2. Pour the soda in next and watch it foam.

MAKES 1 SERVING

This one, I think, is called a Yink.
He likes to wink, he likes to drink.
He likes to drink, and drink,
*   and drink.*
The thing he likes to drink is ink.
The ink he likes to drink is pink.
He likes to wink and drink pink ink.
SO . . . if you have a lot of ink,
then you should get a Yink, I think.
From *One Fish Two Fish*
Red Fish Blue Fish

Pink Yink Ink Drink

Make sure your Yink is in the pink with this (not really ink) drink using fresh fruit, milk, and honey.

Ingredients

½ pint fresh or ½ cup frozen
    blackberries, thawed
1 cup milk
6 fresh strawberries, green tops
    removed, or ½ cup frozen, thawed
1 teaspoon honey

Directions

1. Put the blackberries in a blender and puree them.
2. Pour into a large glass.
3. Put the milk, strawberries, and honey in the blender and blend.
4. Strain the mixture (optional).
5. Pour the strawberry mixture carefully on top of the blackberries.

MAKES 1 SERVING

Doing little odd jobs, he could be of some aid . . .
Such as selling balloons and the pink lemonade.
I think five hundred gallons will be about right.
And THEN, I'll be ready for Opening Night!

From *If I Ran the Circus*

Circus McGurkus Pink Lemonade

If five hundred gallons sounds like a tad too much, then try this version and make just enough for you. If you decide you want more, then double, triple, or quadruple everything to make a big batch. For different tastes and shades of pink, use other fruit juices, like raspberry, strawberry, or even cranberry.

Ingredients

1 tablespoon sugar or ½ to 2 tablespoons light honey
2 tablespoons hot water
1½ cups cold water
juice of 1 lemon, strained
1 tablespoon black cherry juice

Directions

1. Combine the sugar or honey and the hot water in a tall glass and stir until the sugar or honey dissolves.
2. Add the cold water, lemon juice, and cherry juice and stir.

MAKES 1 SERVING

So, every so often, one puts down his hoop,
Stops hooping and does some quick snooping for soup.
That's why they are known as the Hoop-Soup-Snoop Group.

From *Dr. Seuss's Sleep Book*

Hoop-Soup-Snoop Group Potato Soup

Soup is good for spooning and sipping, and this creamy potato soup is worth jumping through a few hoops for, especially with its toppings of croutons, cheese, and bacon—and more, if you want.

Ingredients

1 pound potatoes, peeled and cut into several pieces
¼ cup chopped onion
6 cups water
2 teaspoons salt
2 cups whole milk
½ teaspoon freshly ground black pepper
½ cup grated cheddar cheese
4 slices crisply cooked bacon, crumbled
1 cup croutons
½ cup minced green onion (optional)

Directions

1. In a large saucepan, combine the potatoes, onion, and water and 1 teaspoon of salt. Bring to a boil over high heat. Cover, reduce the heat to medium, and cook until the potatoes are tender, about 20 minutes.
2. Drain the potatoes and return them to the hot saucepan. Mash them with a potato masher.
3. Stir the milk into the mashed potatoes and return to medium heat, stirring, until the soup is well blended and hot, about 5 minutes. Taste and add salt and pepper as desired.
4. Put the cheese, bacon, and croutons and, if you want, the green onion in separate small bowls to accompany the soup.

MAKES 4 SERVINGS

*What do Italians
call macaroni?
They call macaroni* MACARONI.
From *The Cat's Quizzer*

Cat's Mac and Cheese

The Cat, as you know, is full of very tricky tricks. And this trick of stuffing pasta with cheese is one that you can do with ease!

Ingredients

15 ounces ricotta cheese

3 tablespoons minced shallots

½ cup chopped parsley

1 egg yolk

2 teaspoons salt

1 teaspoon freshly ground black pepper

½ cup freshly grated Parmesan cheese

8 ounces extra-large penne, rigatoni, or shell pasta

2½ tablespoons butter

1½ tablespoons all-purpose flour

1½ cups whole milk

3 tablespoons fresh bread crumbs

Directions

1. In a large bowl, combine the ricotta, shallots, parsley, egg yolk, and Parmesan cheese, half of the salt, and half of the black pepper. Mix until smooth, about 2 minutes.

2. Cook the pasta as directed on the package. Drain and rinse with cold water until cool enough to handle.

3. Cut off a corner of a sealable plastic bag and fill it half full with the stuffing. Insert the cut-off tip into each piece of pasta and squeeze, repeating until all the pasta is filled. (You can use a spoon and your fingers instead if you want.)

4. Preheat the oven to 400°F.

5. In a small saucepan, melt 2 tablespoons of the butter over medium heat.

When it foams, remove it from the heat and add the flour slowly, whisking to make a roux, or paste.

6. Return the pan to the heat and whisk in the milk, extremely slowly.

7. Reduce the heat to low and simmer, stirring often, until the sauce is thick enough to coat the back of a spoon and the taste of the flour has gone, about 15 minutes. Stir in the remaining salt and pepper.

8. Into an 8-by-8-inch casserole or baking dish (about 3 inches deep), ladle enough sauce just to cover the bottom. Spread out one-third of the stuffed pasta, then pour one-third of the sauce over it. Repeat twice with the remaining pasta and sauce.

9. In a small frying pan over medium heat, melt the remaining ½ tablespoon of butter and add the bread crumbs, stirring until the bread crumbs are toasted, about 2 minutes. Put them on top of the pasta.

10. Put in the oven and bake until lightly golden, about 15 to 20 minutes.

MAKES 4 SERVINGS

We took a look. We saw a Nook.
On his head he had a hook.
On his hook he had a book.
On his book was "How to Cook."

From *One Fish Two Fish Red Fish Blue Fish*

Nook Hook Cook Book Dogs

Make like a Nook, and put your dogs on sticks, not hooks, to roast them. Pick oak or pecan or hickory or pine sticks—just soak them in water first. If you don't pick sticks, pick long-handled barbecue forks instead.

Ingredients

8 beef or turkey frankfurters

8 oak, pecan, hickory, or pine sticks, about 3 feet long, soaked in water (long-handled barbecue forks may be substituted)

1 large can (1 pound, 12 ounces) Boston baked beans

2 ounces ricotta cheese

4 black olives, pitted

Directions

1. Place each frankfurter on a stick or barbecue fork.
2. Prepare a wood or charcoal fire in a fire pit or barbecue, or heat a gas grill. Hold the frankfurters over the heat, being careful not to get too close. Cook, turning, until the skin bubbles and browns, about 5 to 7 minutes.
3. Push the frankfurters off the sticks or forks with a small fork. Set aside.
4. Put the beans in a saucepan and cook them over medium heat, stirring, until warm all the way through, about 7 minutes.
5. Divide the beans among four bowls, add two roasted frankfurters to each bowl, and top with a spoonful of the ricotta and an olive.

MAKES 4 TO 6 SERVINGS

When a fox is
in the bottle where
the tweetle beetles battle
with their paddles
in a puddle on a
noodle-eating poodle,
THIS is what they call . . .
. . . a tweetle beetle
noodle poodle bottled
paddled muddled duddled
fuddled wuddled
fox in socks, sir!

From *Fox in Socks*

Noodle-Eating-Poodle Noodles

Squiggly, wiggly pasta in weird shapes is the choice of oodles of noodle-eating poodles, preferably wuddled with puddles of butter and cheese before being paddled onto plates.

Ingredients

2 quarts water
1 teaspoon salt
10 ounces fusilli pasta
2 tablespoons butter or extra-virgin olive oil
⅓ cup freshly grated Parmesan cheese

Directions

1. In a pasta pot or other large pot, bring the water to a boil. Add ½ teaspoon of the salt, then the pasta. Cook until tender, about 12 to 13 minutes. Drain.
2. Put the pasta in a bowl and add the butter or olive oil and the remaining ½ teaspoon salt.
3. Using large spoons or forks, turn the pasta over and over until it is coated with the butter or olive oil.
4. Add about a third of the cheese, then turn the pasta again. Sprinkle with the remaining cheese and serve.
MAKES 4 SERVINGS

*At our house
we open cans.
We have to open
many cans.
And that is why
we have a Zans.
A Zans for cans
is very good.
Have you a Zans for cans?
You should.*

From *One Fish Two Fish Red Fish Blue Fish*

Zans' Cans Chili

Even if you don't have a Zans—and few do because of the bans—you should still try to make the Zans chili from cans.

Ingredients

15½-ounce can kidney beans
15½-ounce can pinto beans
14½-ounce can diced tomatoes with sweet
   onions and roasted garlic or similar
1 pound ground turkey or lean beef
½ teaspoon salt
¼ teaspoon freshly ground black pepper
1 teaspoon paprika
¼ teaspoon chili powder, or more if
   desired
⅔ cup grated mild cheddar cheese
¼ cup sour cream
4 sprigs cilantro

Directions

1. Drain the beans and put them in a large saucepan with the seasoned tomatoes. Bring to a simmer over medium heat, stirring occasionally. Simmer until the beans are heated through and flavors have blended, about 7 to 10 minutes.

2. Heat a frying pan over medium heat and crumble the turkey or beef into it. Season with the salt, pepper, paprika, and chili powder. Cook until browned, stirring occasionally, about 7 to 10 minutes.

3. Stir the seasoned meat into the beans.

4. Divide the chili among 4 bowls. Top each with cheese, then sour cream, and stick a cilantro sprig in the middle.

MAKES 4 SERVINGS

Do the Japanese eat with pogo sticks or joss sticks?
Pogo sticks they jump on. Joss sticks they burn.
They eat with CHOP STICKS.

From *The Cat's Quizzer*

Cat's Sticks Mix

Pogo sticks are no-go sticks, so use chopsticks—or a fork or a spoon—to eat the Cat's bowl of rice and carrots and corn. If you want, you can make it with broccoli or cabbage or sweet red peppers or asparagus.

Ingredients

2 cups nonfat chicken broth
1 cup long-grain white rice
16 mini-carrots
15-ounce can baby corn
¼ cup chopped cilantro (optional)

Directions

1. Put the chicken broth in a saucepan and bring to a boil.
2. Add the rice, bring back to a boil, then reduce the heat to low and cover.
3. Cook without stirring until the rice is tender, about 20 minutes.
4. While the rice is cooking, slice the carrots and corn into thin rounds.
5. Divide the rice among four bowls and top each with the carrots and corn.
6. Serve sprinkled with cilantro if you want.

MAKES 4 SERVINGS

*Daisy-Head burgers,
And Daisy-Head drinks.
Daisy-Head stockings,
And Daisy-Head sinks.
Daisy-Head buttons,
And Daisy-Head bows.
Mayzie was famous,
The star of her shows.*

From *Daisy-Head Mayzie*

Daisy-Head Mayzie Burgers

Make these big, juicy hamburgers the Daisy-Head way—that is, with a gingerbread-daisy dessert stuck right on top. You can make the cookies a day ahead if you want.

Ingredients for Hamburgers

12 lean ground-beef patties
1 teaspoon salt
1 teaspoon black pepper
6 sesame hamburger buns plus 6 more bun bottoms
mayonnaise (optional)
mustard (optional)
ketchup (optional)
relish (optional)
24 slices of American or Swiss cheese
12 large lettuce leaves
2 large tomatoes, sliced (optional)
1 large onion, thinly sliced (optional)
sliced sweet or dill pickles (optional)

Directions for Hamburgers

1. Sprinkle each patty with a little of the salt and pepper.
2. Preheat the oven to 350°F.
3. Put the buns on a baking sheet cut side down, and heat until warm, about 10 minutes. Remove and set aside.
4. Preheat broiler.
5. Put the patties on a broiler pan and set about 4 inches from the heat source. Broil until brown, about 4 minutes. Turn and broil the other side until brown, about 4 minutes.
6. Spread the 12 bun bottoms with whatever you like—mayonnaise, mustard, ketchup, relish—or leave them plain if you prefer.
7. Put a patty on each bun bottom, then 2 pieces of cheese, 1 piece of lettuce, and, if you want, a slice of tomato, a slice of onion, and even pickles.

8. Stack one of these creations on top of another. Repeat until you have 6 double-stacked hamburgers. Now spread whatever you want on the inside of the 6 top buns and place on the stacked hamburgers.

9. Stick a daisy cookie onto the top of each hamburger.

MAKES 6 HAMBURGERS

Ingredients for Cookies

1 stick of butter at room temperature
½ cup firmly packed light brown sugar
½ cup light molasses
3 cups all-purpose flour
1 teaspoon baking soda
¼ teaspoon ground cloves
½ teaspoon ground cinnamon
½ teaspoon grated nutmeg
1 teaspoon ground ginger
½ teaspoon salt
⅓ cup milk

Ingredients for Icing

2 egg whites
4¼ cups (1 pound) confectioners' sugar
1 teaspoon water (optional)
green food coloring
yellow food coloring

Directions for Cookies

1. Trace or draw the cookie shape shown above. Tape it onto cardboard and cut it out to make your cookie pattern.

2. Preheat oven to 350°F. Using 1 teaspoon of butter, grease a large baking sheet.

3. In a large bowl, using an electric mixer, beat the remaining butter and the sugar until light and fluffy. Beat in the molasses until well blended.

4. In a medium bowl, combine the flour, baking soda, cloves, cinnamon, nutmeg, ginger, and salt. Whisk them together to mix well.

5. Add half the flour mixture to the butter mixture and beat until well blended. Beat in about ¼ cup of milk, then add the remaining flour mixture, beating it well. If it is crumbly, add a little extra milk as needed. Gather the dough into a ball and pack firmly together.

6. On a well-floured surface, roll the dough until it is ½ inch thick.

7. Lay the flower pattern on the dough and cut around it with a knife to make each cookie. Transfer the cutouts to the baking sheet.

8. Bake for 7 or 8 minutes or until the cookies are puffed and spring back when pushed with your finger. Transfer to a wire rack to cool.

Directions for Icing

1. In a large bowl, using an electric mixer, beat the egg whites and 4 cups of confectioners' sugar until very stiff, about 10 minutes. If the icing is too stiff, add a teaspoon of water. If too thin, add about ¼ cup more of confectioners' sugar.

2. Put about 4 tablespoons of the icing in a bowl and add a few drops of green food coloring.

3. Put about 2 tablespoons of the icing in another bowl and add a few drops of yellow food coloring.

4. Using a knife or a small spatula, ice the daisy cookies.

MAKES ABOUT 16 COOKIES

On a mountain,
*   halfway between Reno and Rome,*
We have a machine
*   in a plexiglass dome*
Which listens and looks
*   into everyone's home.*
And whenever it sees
*   a new sleeper go flop,*
It jiggles and lets
*   a new Biggel-Ball drop.*
        From *Dr. Seuss's Sleep Book*

Biggel-Balls

Biggel-Balls are bite-size cheese balls—your choice of cheese, rolled in nuts and seeds. Biggel-Balls will boggle all!

Ingredients

5 ounces grated mild cheddar, Monterey Jack, or other cheese
1 tablespoon sour cream
1 tablespoon butter at room temperature
1 tablespoon minced chives
¼ teaspoon salt
⅓ to ½ cup poppy or sesame seeds, chopped green pumpkin seeds, chopped
    pistachios or pecans, or other seeds or nuts

Directions

1. In a food processor, combine the cheese, sour cream, butter, chives, and salt and process until smooth, about 1 minute.
2. Using your hands, shape the mixture into bite-size balls. Place on a tray lined with aluminum foil and refrigerate until firm, about 1 hour.
3. Spread the seeds or nuts on a plate and roll the balls in them.
Makes about 18 balls

All those NUPBOARDS
in the CUPBOARDS.
They're good fun
to have about.

From *There's a Wocket in My Pocket!*

Nupboards' Nuggets

Nupboards like to eat Nuggets—a clumpy, bumpy cross between nut brittle and trail mix, made out of items you can find in your cupboards.

Ingredients

2½ cups uncooked oatmeal (not quick-cooking)
1 cup green pumpkin seeds
1 cup whole almonds
½ cup light cooking oil, such as canola or sunflower
½ cup honey
3 tablespoons dark brown sugar
1 teaspoon cinnamon
1 teaspoon almond extract

Directions

1. Preheat the oven to 300°F.
2. In a large bowl, combine the oatmeal, pumpkin seeds, almonds, oil, honey, brown sugar, cinnamon, and almond extract and mix well, using your hands if necessary.
3. Spread the mixture on a large baking sheet and bake until browned, stirring from time to time to prevent burning, about 45 minutes to 1 hour.
4. Remove from the oven. Using a fork or spatula, push the mixture together. Let cool completely, then break up into clumps. (There will be some unclumped bits that you can use for granola or trail snacks.) May be stored in an airtight container for up to three weeks.
MAKES ABOUT 4 CUPS

Fritz feeds Fred and Fred feeds Fritz.
Fred feeds Fritz with ritzy Fred food.
Fritz feeds Fred with ritzy Fritz food.
And Fritz, when fed, has often said,
"I'm a Fred-fed Fritz.
Fred's a Fritz-fed Fred."

From *Oh Say Can You Say?*

"Fritz-Fed Fred" Food Feast

Fred food is fun to make and to eat. No cooking required for Fred's ritzy pickles. Keep them in the refrigerator until ready to feed a Fritz or yourself. You can pickle all kinds of fun food, like radishes, carrots, beans, snap peas, okra, and more.

Ingredients

1 cup water
1 cup white distilled vinegar
    (5 percent acidity)
2 tablespoons sugar
2 tablespoons canning salt
1 teaspoon whole peppercorns
1 teaspoon mustard seeds
1 pound small pickling cucumbers
4 large sprigs fresh dill, coarsely
    chopped (about 1 cup)

Directions

1. In a large bowl, combine the water, vinegar, sugar, salt, peppercorns, and mustard seeds. Stir well to dissolve the salt and sugar.

2. Put the cucumbers in a bowl and pour the vinegar mixture over them. Put in the refrigerator for 6 hours.

3. Put the fresh dill in a one-pint wide-mouth canning jar. Put in the cucumbers, then pour the vinegar mixture over them, covering them to within half an inch of the jar's rim. Cover and refrigerate two weeks to allow the flavors to blend before eating. You can keep the pickles in the refrigerator for up to two months.

MAKES 1 PINT

And, while we are at it, consider the Schlottz,
the Crumple-horn, Web-footed, Green-bearded Schlottz,
whose tail is entailed with un-solvable knots.

From *Did I Ever Tell You How Lucky You Are?*

Schlottz's Knots

Stretching the dough into long, droopy ropes will give you plenty of tail to twist and shape into Schlottz-like knots.

Ingredients

11-ounce package of
    bread-stick dough
    (8 sticks dough)
2 tablespoons water
1 tablespoon coarse sea salt

Directions

1. Preheat the oven to 375°F.
2. Separate the dough into 8 sticks.
3. Stretch one of the dough sticks until it is 2 feet long and about as big around as two pencils.
4. Tie the dough stick into one, two, or three loose knots and lay it on a nonstick baking sheet or a baking sheet lined with parchment paper.
5. Repeat with the remaining dough sticks, using a second baking sheet if needed.
6. Brush each knotted tail with water, then sprinkle with a little of the sea salt.
7. Bake until golden brown and firm, about 15 to 20 minutes.

MAKES 8 PRETZELS

Variation: For easy cheesy knots, sprinkle the pretzels with finely grated Parmesan or Gruyère during the last few minutes of baking, letting the cheese become slightly golden.

SNACK
SNACK
Eat a snack.
Eat a snack
with Brown and Black.
From *Hop on Pop*

Brown and Black's Snack

Corn bread squares make a fine snack. Top them with brown beans or black ones for a Brown and Black's Snack. If you don't want to make your own corn bread, try the beans with store-bought corn bread muffins or with toasted bagels or warm flour tortillas. To make a full meal instead of a snack, fry up some ground beef to add to the black beans, and add sausage instead of bacon to the baked beans. If you want to cook your own black beans, cook one cup of beans in six cups of water, along with a teaspoon of salt, a chopped onion, and a bay leaf. When they are tender, after about one and a half hours, add more salt and some pepper to taste.

Ingredients

butter
1 cup yellow cornmeal
1 cup all-purpose flour
1 teaspoon sugar
½ teaspoon salt
1 tablespoon baking powder
1 teaspoon dried thyme
1 cup whole milk
⅓ cup light vegetable oil, such as canola or sunflower
1 large egg
kernels cut from 1 ear white or yellow corn
15-ounce can of black beans or Boston baked beans
8 ounces fresh salsa (for black beans) or 10 crispy bacon strips (for baked beans)

Directions for Corn Bread

1. Preheat the oven to 400°F. Using the butter, grease an 8-inch square baking pan.
2. In a large bowl, mix together the cornmeal, flour, sugar, salt, baking powder, and thyme with a whisk.
3. In a small bowl, mix together the milk, oil, and egg until well blended, about 2 minutes.
4. Pour into the cornmeal mixture and whisk until blended, about 40 seconds. Do not overmix.
5. Pour the mixture into the pan and sprinkle with the corn kernels.

6. Bake until the corn bread is puffed and golden, about 20 to 25 minutes. A knife or wooden toothpick inserted into the center should come out clean.

7. Remove and let stand 10 minutes before cutting into sixteen 2-inch squares.

Directions for Beans

1. Pour the beans into a saucepan. Place over medium heat and stir until the beans are hot, about 7 minutes.

2. Stir 1 tablespoon of salsa into the black beans or stir two pieces of crumbled bacon into the brown beans.

3. Cut two squares of corn bread into top and bottom halves. Put the bottom halves in the middle of a plate, cut sides up.

4. Top with the beans. (They can spill over the sides.) Put the top halves over the beans, cut sides down.

5. Spoon a little salsa over the black beans or crumble a slice of bacon on top of the brown beans. Repeat with the remaining squares of corn bread.

MAKES 8 SERVINGS

And, under the trees, I saw Brown Bar-ba-loots
frisking about in their Bar-ba-loot suits
as they played in the shade and ate Truffula Fruits.
From *The Lorax*

Brown Bar-ba-loots' Truffula Fruits

Truffula Fruits are not readily found, but you can make your own version and discover why the Bar-ba-loots went Bar-ba-loopy for these uncommon fruits.

Ingredients

12 to 16 strawberries, with long stems if possible

8 to 12 ounces strawberry yogurt

Directions

1. Place three or four strawberries on each of four plates, along with a small bowl of yogurt.

2. Dip the strawberries in the yogurt.

MAKES 4 TO 5 SERVINGS

I'll go to the far-away Mountains of Tobsk
Near the River of Nobsk, and I'll bring back an Obsk,
A sort of a kind of a Thing-a-ma-Bobsk
Who only eats rhubarb and corn-on-the-cobsk.

From *If I Ran the Zoo*

River of Nobsk Corn-off-the-Cobsk

What could be simpler than corn-off-the-cobsk, all popped and ready to season and eat? The Obsk suggests flavoring it with a spicy red cheese Thing-a-ma-Bobsk. Your tummy will throbsk with joy!

Ingredients

6 cups popped, unseasoned popcorn
2 tablespoons extra-virgin olive oil or other light cooking oil, such as canola
    or sunflower
½ cup freshly grated Parmesan cheese
1 teaspoon paprika
¼ to ½ teaspoon chili powder
½ teaspoon salt

Directions

1. Put the popped corn in a large bowl and add the oil. Turn well to coat the corn.
2. Sprinkle with the cheese, paprika, chili powder, and salt.
Turn well to coat.
MAKES 6 CUPS

She snatched at those berries that grew on that vine.
She gobbled down four, five, six, seven, eight, nine!
And she didn't stop eating, young Gertrude McFuzz,
Till she'd eaten three dozen! That's all that there was.

From "Gertrude McFuzz" in *Yertle the Turtle and Other Stories*

Gertrude McFuzz-y Berries

Gertrude ate three dozen berries, which was a *berry* large amount for her, but these home-frozen treats are so good you can eat more than just a few. Put them in a bowl for a snack, drop them into drinks for a sparkle, or use them as an ice cream topping.

Ingredients

½ cup sugar
3 ounces fresh raspberries
3 ounces fresh blackberries
3 ounces fresh blueberries

Directions

1. Line a baking sheet with aluminum foil.
2. Put the berries, 3 or 4 at a time, into a bowl containing the sugar and turn them around until coated.
3. Put the sugared berries in a single layer on the foil.
4. Freeze until firm, about 30 minutes.
5. The berries may be refrigerated in a plastic bag for up to two weeks.

MAKES ABOUT 65 SUGARED BERRIES

You can learn about ice.
You can learn about mice.
Mice on ice.
And ice on mice. . . .
Nice ice
for sale.
Ten cents a pail.

From *I Can Read with My Eyes Shut!*

Nice Lime Ice (Hold the Mice!)

Without fail, you can use a pail to unveil your limeade—it's for sale! If you have leftover limeade, keep it in the refrigerator to make more ice. And remember to hold the mice!

Ingredients

4 cups water
¾ cup sugar
¼ teaspoon salt
½ cup lime juice (about 6 to 8 limes)

Directions

1. In a saucepan, combine the water, sugar, and salt and bring to a boil over medium heat, stirring often. Boil, continuing to stir, until the sugar has dissolved and a light syrup has formed, about 2 minutes.

2. Remove from the heat, let cool, cover, and refrigerate until well chilled.

3. Combine the syrup with the lime juice in a pitcher or bowl and stir well. Taste and add more sugar if desired.

4. Pour into ice cube trays and freeze until slightly firm, about 45 minutes. Stick a toothpick, pointed side out, into each cube.

Return to the freezer until solid, about 3 hours for small cubes or 4 hours for large ones.

5. To make towers of ice, stick the cubes together using the toothpicks in each.

MAKES 72 LARGE CUBES

If you like to eat potato chips
and chew pork chops on clipper ships,
I suggest that you chew
a few chips and a chop
at Skipper Zipp's Clipper Ship Chip Chop Shop.

From *Oh Say Can You Say?*

Skipper Zipp's Chops and Chips

Nothing could be simpler than Skipper Zipp's clipper ship meal. When the chops are baked juicy and brown, the chips crispy and golden (these are English-style chips—potatoes cut in wedges like big French fries), you're ready to chew. Now, spuds can be cooked different ways, if you want a change. You can bake them whole, for example, right in their skins. Choose a brown russet type, wash it, then rub it with olive oil and put it in the oven with the temperature at 350 degrees. After an hour and fifteen minutes, take it out. It's tender and flaking inside, just right for a pat of butter and salt and pepper, or top it with plain yogurt or sour cream instead. Or with cheese or beans or salsa or spinach. Whatever you like. They're not Zipp's Chips, but they still go great with chops.

Ingredients

4 center-cut pork loin chops, with bone
1 teaspoon salt
½ teaspoon freshly ground black pepper
4 large potatoes, cut lengthwise into 6 wedges
1½ tablespoons extra-virgin olive oil
¼ teaspoon paprika

Directions

1. Preheat the oven to 350°F.
2. Sprinkle half the salt and all the pepper on the chops and put them on a baking sheet. Set aside.
3. Put the potatoes on a baking sheet, then sprinkle them with the olive oil and roll them around. Sprinkle them with the remaining ½ teaspoon salt and the paprika.
4. Put the potatoes in the oven and turn after half an hour.
5. Put the pork chops in the oven when you turn the potatoes. Cook both until the chops are juicy and brown, about 20 to 25 minutes, and the potatoes are golden and tender, about half an hour.
6. Serve hot on a platter.
MAKES 4 SERVINGS

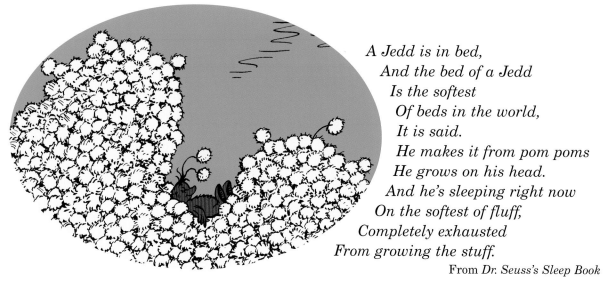

A Jedd is in bed,
And the bed of a Jedd
Is the softest
Of beds in the world,
It is said.
He makes it from pom poms
He grows on his head.
And he's sleeping right now
On the softest of fluff,
Completely exhausted
From growing the stuff.

From *Dr. Seuss's Sleep Book*

Jedd's Bed of Shrimp

Bite-size puffs of coconut-crusted shrimp look just like the fluffy balls on the head of a Jedd. For a fun way to serve these, stick each shrimp on the end of a toothpick, then stick the other end of the toothpick in a whole pineapple.

Ingredients

3 egg whites
½ teaspoon salt
½ teaspoon chili powder (optional)
3 pounds raw rock shrimp or other small shrimp, shelled
8-ounce bag sweetened or unsweetened coconut, fine shred, or substitute
    medium shred
light vegetable oil, such as canola or sunflower
1 whole pineapple (optional)
2 cups purchased fruit salsa (optional)

Directions

1. With an electric beater, beat the egg whites until frothy. Add the salt and, if you want, the chili powder.
2. Dry the shrimp thoroughly with absorbent paper towels.
3. Spread about 1 cup of the coconut on a sheet of wax paper.
4. Line a baking sheet with wax or parchment paper.
5. One by one, dip the shrimp first in the egg whites, then in the coconut, pressing the coconut onto them. Set on the prepared baking sheet.
6. Put a 2½-inch layer of oil in a heavy-bottomed pan. Heat it over medium heat until it sizzles and bubbles when a shrimp is dropped in. Fry all the shrimp until golden, about 3 minutes, then turn with tongs and fry another minute or two. Remove with the tongs to a platter lined with absorbent paper towels. Stick the shrimp in a pineapple with toothpicks if desired.
7. Serve with fruit salsa.

MAKES 8 TO 10 SERVINGS

And you'll now meet the Foon!
The Remarkable Foon
Who eats sizzling hot pebbles
that fall off the moon!
And the reason he likes them
red hot, it appears,
Is he greatly enjoys
blowing smoke from his ears.

From *If I Ran the Circus*

Remarkable Foon's Sizzling Hot Pebbles

The Remarkable Foon's Sizzling Hot Pebbles are really red beans. The Foon cooked them with spices and onions and added hot sausage, then mixed it all up with white rice. The Remarkable Foon will put you in a swoon!

Ingredients

8 cups water
2 pounds smoked ham hocks
3 stalks celery, chopped
1 small onion, diced
1 large green bell pepper, seeded, ribs removed, and chopped
4 to 6 cloves garlic, minced
2 bay leaves
1 teaspoon dried thyme
1 teaspoon dried oregano
1 teaspoon freshly ground black pepper
½ to 1 teaspoon chili powder
1 pound small red beans, soaked overnight in cold water
1 pound fully cooked smoked sausages, spicy or not, cut into ¼-inch-thick slices
salt (optional)

Directions

1. In a large pot, combine the water, ham hocks, celery, onion, bell pepper, garlic, bay leaves, thyme, oregano, black pepper, and chili powder. Bring to a boil over high heat, cover, and reduce the heat to low. Simmer, stirring from time to time, until the ham hocks are tender and slightly pulled away from the bone, about 1½ hours.

2. Remove the ham hocks and let them cool.

3. Drain the presoaked beans and add them to the pot. Bring to a boil over high heat, cover, and reduce the heat to low. Simmer, stirring from time to time, until the beans are tender, about 2 hours.

4. Remove the rind from the ham hocks and discard. Remove the meat and chop it. Add it to the beans.

5. Stir in the slices of sausage and cook until warmed through, about 10 minutes.

6. Add salt if needed.

7. To serve, mix the hot pebbles up with the white rice.

MAKES 6 TO 8 SERVINGS

Do you like fresh fish?
It's just fine at Finney's Diner.
Finney also has some fresher fish
that's fresher and much finer.
But his best fish is his freshest fish
and Finney says with pride,
"The finest fish at Finney's
is my freshest fish, French-fried!"
From *Oh Say Can You Say?*

Finney's Freshest Fish

Fresh fish is really the best you can get, and fresher and freshest are still better yet. Just pack it with a crunchy crust and bake, not fry, until golden and crisp. Serve it with a side of Finney's Coleslaw and Finney's Finest Dilly Dip.

Ingredients for Fish

2 eggs

1 cup almonds

½ cup toasted oat cereal, such as Cheerios

2½ tablespoons extra-virgin olive oil

4 fillets of a firm fish, such as red snapper, sea bass, or cod, cut into 1-inch-wide strips

1 teaspoon salt

1 teaspoon freshly ground black pepper

Ingredients for Coleslaw

½ small red cabbage, thinly sliced

½ small green cabbage, thinly sliced

2 carrots, coarsely grated

¼ cup rice wine vinegar

2 tablespoons canola, sunflower, or other light cooking oil

2 to 3 tablespoons honey

¼ to ½ teaspoon salt

¼ teaspoon freshly ground black pepper

Ingredients for Dip

¼ cup mayonnaise

1 tablespoon whole milk

1 teaspoon cider vinegar

1 teaspoon Dijon-style mustard

3 tablespoons minced sweet pickles

2 teaspoons minced onions

1 teaspoon pickle juice

Directions for Fish

1. Preheat the oven to 450°F.

2. In a small bowl, beat the eggs until frothy. Pour into a pie plate or another shallow plate.

3. Chop the almonds and the toasted oat cereal in a blender or with a knife to make a crumblike mixture. Put it on a sheet of wax paper or aluminum foil.

4. Use a tablespoon of the olive oil to grease a baking sheet.

5. Pat the fish dry with paper towels. Dip it in the eggs, then lay it atop the almonds and toasted oat cereal, pressing down. Gently turn it over and press the crumbs into the other side. Lay on the baking sheet and let stand 15 minutes to set the crust.

6. Sprinkle the fish with the salt and pepper and drizzle with the remaining olive oil.

7. Bake until the fish is opaque and easily flakes with a fork, about 15 minutes.

Directions for Coleslaw

1. Put the sliced cabbage in a bowl with the carrots.

2. In a small bowl, combine the vinegar, oil, honey, salt, and pepper and mix well.

3. Pour the mixture over the cabbage and carrots and toss well to coat.

Directions for Dip

In a bowl, combine the mayonnaise, milk, vinegar, mustard, pickles, onions, and pickle juice and mix well.

MAKES 4 SERVINGS

They would feast on Who-*pudding,*
and rare Who-*roast-beast*
Which was something the Grinch
couldn't stand in the least!
From *How the Grinch Stole Christmas!*

Who-Roast-Beast

This roast-beast is a chicken, whose dramatic
Who look is made by tucking mushrooms under
its skin—just the thing to make a
Grinch flinch, for the Grinch
hates all things *Who*.

Ingredients

1 fryer chicken,
   3 to 3½ pounds
2 tablespoons extra-virgin
   olive oil
1 teaspoon salt
1 teaspoon freshly ground black pepper
1 pound white or brown button mushrooms, thinly sliced
1½ tablespoons minced fresh sage, plus 4 sprigs

Directions

1. Preheat the oven to 350°F.
2. Rub the chicken with 1 tablespoon of olive oil, ½ teaspoon of salt, and ½ teaspoon of pepper.
3. Mix the mushrooms in a bowl with the remaining salt and pepper and the minced sage.
4. Lay the chicken on its back with its legs facing you. Slip your hand between the skin and the meat of the chicken breast. Gently move your hand under the skin toward the neck of the chicken, loosening the skin and making a pocket for the mushrooms. Be careful not to tear the skin. Also slip your hand as far down around the thighs as you can.
5. Take a few mushrooms at a time and, with your fingers, slide them under the skin toward the neck, packing them tightly together in a single layer. Repeat until all the mushrooms are used and the chicken's skin looks lumpy.
6. Put the sage sprigs in the chicken cavity.
7. With kitchen string, tie the drumsticks together across the cavity.
8. Place the chicken on a rack in a roasting pan. Roast until the juice at the thigh runs clear when you pierce the meat with a knife, about 1 hour and 15 minutes.
9. Remove from the oven and let stand 10 to 15 minutes before carving.
MAKES 4 SERVINGS

They'll fix up a dish that is just to his taste;
Three chicken croquettes made of library paste,
Then sprinkled with peanut shucks, pickled and spiced,
Then baked at 600 degrees and then iced.

From If I Ran the Zoo

Kartoom Croquettes

A beast called the Natch, who lives in Kartoom, has always stayed in his cave, refusing to come out. But Gerald McGrew, who plans to catch unusual creatures for his zoo, decides to lure him out with pickled, peanut-sprinkled chicken croquettes. Will these delicacies work? *Natch!*

Ingredients

2 cups finely chopped cooked chicken

4 tablespoons bread crumbs

2 tablespoons minced green onions

1 teaspoon chili paste

½ teaspoon salt

2 small eggs

1 cup finely chopped unsalted peanuts

1½ tablespoons light vegetable oil, such as canola or sunflower

4 sprigs of cilantro and 8 baby carrots (optional)

Directions

1. Preheat the oven to 400°F.

2. In a bowl, mix together the chicken, bread crumbs, green onions, chili paste, salt, and eggs to make a thick paste. With your hands, divide the mixture into twelve equal parts, then shape them into logs.

3. Put the chopped peanuts on a plate and gently roll each log in the peanuts to coat it.

4. Place the logs on a nonstick baking sheet or a baking sheet lined with parchment paper.

5. Drizzle the top of each log with a little oil.

6. Bake until golden brown and firm to the touch, about 15 to 20 minutes.

To Serve

Put three croquettes on each plate. Garnish with the cilantro and carrots if you wish.

MAKES 4 SERVINGS

Some of them are very friendly.
Like the
YOT
in the
POT.
But
that
YOTTLE
in
the
BOTTLE!
Some are friendly. Some are NOT.
From *There's a Wocket in My Pocket!*

Yot in the Pot

Put a lot in your pot, not a Yot. You can put a lot of vegetables, a lot of sausage, even a lot of clams still in their shells. You can use different kinds of sausage and even clams in a can if you want, or shrimp if that's your favorite. Or all of the above so that you've got quite a lot for your pot.

Ingredients

1 teaspoon extra-virgin olive oil
2 mild Italian sausages, cut into 1-inch pieces
2 tablespoons chopped onions
1 clove garlic, chopped
½ cup canned tomatoes, chopped, with their juice
4 cups chicken broth
½ teaspoon dried oregano
2 large potatoes, peeled and chopped into bite-size pieces
2 ears of corn, with kernels cut off the cob
1 pound clams in their shells (one 9-to-10-ounce can whole clams with juice
    may be substituted)
salt and pepper (optional)

Directions

1. Heat the olive oil in a soup pot over medium heat. Add the sausages and cook until browned, about 5 minutes.
2. Add the onions and garlic and stir a minute or two, then add the tomatoes, chicken broth, oregano, and potatoes.
3. Reduce the heat to low and simmer until the potatoes are tender, about 15 minutes.
4. Add the corn and the clams.
5. Cover and cook another 10 minutes. Add salt and pepper if needed.
MAKES 4 SERVINGS

Do you know where I found him? You know where he was?
He was eating a cake in the tub! Yes he was!

From *The Cat in the Hat Comes Back*

Cat in the Hat Tub Cake

The Cat's cake is easy to make, but eating in the tub is difficult, indeed (and very messy).

Ingredients

1 purchased angel food cake
¾ cup heavy whipping cream
¼ cup sugar
¾ cup fresh strawberries, stems
     and leaves removed, or
     frozen, partially thawed,
     plus 5 extra berries

Directions

1. Place the cake on a cake stand or cake plate.
2. Using an electric mixer, beat the whipping cream until it stands in soft peaks.
3. Add the sugar and beat until the cream stands in firm peaks.
4. In a blender, puree the strawberries. Using a spatula, gently fold them into the whipped cream, which will lose some of its stiffness.
5. With the spatula, generously spread the outside of the cake with the whipped cream. Spoon the remainder into the center, filling it to the brim. Decorate the top with the extra strawberries.
6. Serve immediately, or refrigerate for up to one hour. (Any longer and you run the risk of the whipped cream getting oozy.) Cut the cake into wedges. Add another scoop of whipped cream to each wedge.
MAKES 10 TO 12 SERVINGS

The Blindfolded Bowman from Brigger-ba-Root,
The world's sharpest sharpshooter. Look at him shoot!
Through the holes in four doughnuts! Two hairs on a worm!
And the knees of three birds without making them squirm!

From *If I Ran the Circus*

Brigger-ba-Root Doughnut Shoot

Here are cake doughnuts to decorate *your* way, with peanut butter or pickles or candy or cheese—whatever you like, whatever you please. Try making them from scratch, the old-fashioned way, or buy plain ones ready-made.

Ingredients for Doughnuts

1 tablespoon cider vinegar
1 cup milk
3½ cups all-purpose flour
3 teaspoons baking powder
1 teaspoon baking soda
½ teaspoon salt
2 tablespoons butter at room temperature
1 cup sugar
2 eggs
½ teaspoon vanilla
light vegetable oil, such as canola or sunflower

Ingredients for White Chocolate Cutouts

4 ounces white chocolate
⅛ teaspoon pink powdered food coloring
⅛ teaspoon blue powdered food coloring

Ingredients for Cream Cheese Frosting

8 ounces whipped cream cheese
3 raspberries

Directions for Doughnuts

1. In a small bowl, combine the milk and cider vinegar.
2. In a large bowl, mix together 3½ cups of flour and the baking powder, baking soda, and salt with a whisk.
3. In another large bowl, using a wooden spoon or an electric mixer, stir the butter and sugar until smooth.
4. Beat the eggs and vanilla into the butter-and-sugar mixture.
5. Add about one-third of the flour mixture, then add ⅓ cup of the milk-and-vinegar mixture and stir just until blended. Repeat until all the ingredients are used.

6. Cover the dough and refrigerate for 1 hour.

7. Generously sprinkle a work surface with flour. Dip your hands in the flour, then remove one-third of the dough and pat it out to about half an inch thick. Using a 3-inch-diameter cookie cutter, cut out circles. With a knife, cut out a small circle in the middle of each large circle.

8. In a heavy-bottomed saucepan, heat 3 inches of vegetable oil over medium heat. When it is hot, use a spatula to slide two or three of the dough circles into the oil, one at a time. Cook until brown on the underside, about 45 seconds to 1 minute. Turn with the spatula and cook the other side until brown, about another 45 seconds. Place on paper towels to drain.

9. Repeat until all the doughnuts are made.

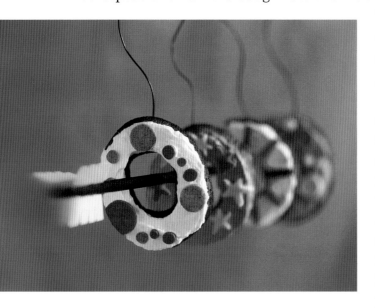

Directions for White Chocolate Cutouts

(These can be made the day before and kept in the refrigerator.)

1. Break the chocolate into pieces and put them in a metal bowl. Half fill a saucepan with water and place over medium heat. When the water is hot, put the bowl on top. When the chocolate begins to melt, in about 1 minute, stir until completely melted, about another 2 or 3 minutes.

2. Holding the metal bowl with a pot holder, pour one-third of the melted chocolate onto a sheet of wax paper. Using a spatula, spread it to a thickness of ⅛ to ¼ inch. Pour another one-third into a small bowl, stir in ⅛ teaspoon of pink powdered food coloring, and spread as above onto a sheet of wax paper. Stir ⅛ teaspoon of blue powdered food coloring into the remaining chocolate and spread it on a sheet of wax paper. Let all the chocolate sheets stand for 10 minutes, then put them in the refrigerator for 30 minutes.

3. Using small cookie cutters or a knife, cut out fun shapes from the chocolate sheets. Put back in the refrigerator until you're ready to decorate the doughnuts, as the chocolate melts quickly.

Directions for Cream Cheese Frosting

1. Scoop 5 tablespoons of the whipped cream cheese into a bowl. Add the raspberries and mash with a fork to flavor the cheese.

2. While the doughnuts are still slightly warm, use a knife or spatula to top them with the plain and flavored cream cheese.

3. Decorate them with the chocolate cutouts.

MAKES ABOUT 18 DOUGHNUTS

And here comes your cake! Cooked by Snookers and Snookers,
The Official Katroo Happy Birthday Cake Cookers.

From *Happy Birthday to You!*

Katroo "Happy Birthday to You" Cake

For your delectation, the cookers at Snookers and Snookers have cooked up this rich, dark, moist, brownie-like cake.

Ingredients for Cake

4 ounces plus ½ teaspoon butter at room temperature

1 cup sugar

2 eggs, beaten

1 teaspoon vanilla

¾ cup all-purpose flour

⅛ teaspoon salt

4 ounces semisweet baking chocolate,
    at least 62 percent cacao

Ingredients for Buttercream Frosting

1 ounce butter at room
    temperature

1 cup tightly packed
    confectioners' sugar

⅛ teaspoon salt

½ teaspoon vanilla

1 drop yellow food coloring
    (optional)

1 tablespoon heavy cream

Ingredients for White Icing

1 egg white

⅛ teaspoon cream of tartar

3 tablespoons cold water

¾ cup sugar

1 teaspoon corn syrup

½ teaspoon vanilla

Directions for Cake

1. Preheat the oven to 350°F.

2. Put the 4 ounces of butter in a large mixing bowl. Using an electric mixer, beat it until it is creamy and fluffy, about 1 minute.

3. Add the sugar and beat until well blended, about 1 minute. Add the eggs and vanilla and beat again until well blended, about 1 minute.

4. Add ¼ cup of flour with the salt and beat well. Add the remaining flour in two batches, beating well after each one.

5. Break or cut the chocolate into pieces and put them in the top of a double boiler over boiling water. Cook, stirring, until the chocolate has melted, about 2 minutes. Add it to the cake batter and beat until well blended and creamy.

6. Line an 8-inch round cake pan with a piece of aluminum foil, allowing the edges to overlap the pan. Lightly grease the foil with the remaining butter and pour in the batter, spreading it evenly across the top with a spatula.

7. Bake until it has puffed and a wooden toothpick inserted in the middle comes out clean, 20 to 25 minutes.

8. Remove to a cake rack and let cool. When cool, lift the cake out using the edges of the foil. Peel off the foil and place the cake on a cake stand or cake plate.

Directions for Buttercream Frosting

1. Put the butter in a large bowl. Using an electric mixer, beat until creamy and fluffy, about 1 minute. Add the sugar a little at a time.

2. Add the salt and vanilla and beat until creamy.

3. Add the food coloring if desired, then the cream, a little bit at a time. Stop when the frosting is easy to spread.

4. Using a spatula, carefully spread the frosting all along the sides of the cake in a nice, thick layer.

Directions for White Icing

1. Put the egg white, cream of tartar, cold water, sugar, and corn syrup in the top of a double boiler over boiling water for about 7 minutes.

2. Using an electric hand mixer, beat until the icing is stiff enough to stand in soft peaks. Remove from the heat and stir in the vanilla.

3. Immediately spread the top of the cake with the icing, using a spatula and creating thick swirls. Swirl some of the icing down over the buttercream frosting to make a true Katroo cake.

MAKES 10 SERVINGS

Now, the Star-Belly Sneetches
Had bellies with stars.
The Plain-Belly Sneetches
Had none upon thars.

From *The Sneetches and Other Stories*

Sneetch Treats

Whether Star-Belly or Plain-Belly, when Sneetches get together for a marshmallow roast, they all eat Sneetch Treats, which are Sneetch-style s'mores. To toast the marshmallows, use sticks or long-handled barbecue forks, just like for the Nook Hook Cook Book Dogs. Make the cookies ahead so they're all ready, or use store-bought cookies.

Ingredients for Oatmeal Cookies

8 ounces butter, melted
1½ cups brown sugar
2 eggs
1 teaspoon vanilla
1½ cups all-purpose flour
1 teaspoon baking soda
½ teaspoon salt
3½ cups uncooked
   one-minute oatmeal
½ cup chopped walnuts
1 cup golden raisins

Ingredients for S'more Filling

3 chocolate bars, 3½ ounces each, broken into squares
24 marshmallows
oak, pecan, hickory, or pine sticks, about 3 feet long, soaked in water
   (long-handled barbecue forks may be substituted)

Directions for Oatmeal Cookies

1. Preheat the oven to 350°F.
2. Combine the melted butter, brown sugar, eggs, and vanilla in a bowl and mix well.
3. In another bowl, combine the flour, baking soda, and salt and mix with a whisk, then add to the butter mixture.
4. Add the oatmeal, walnuts, and raisins and mix well.
5. Drop the cookie batter onto ungreased baking sheets, 1 tablespoon at a time. Flatten slightly with the back of a spatula.
6. Bake until golden and firm, about 12 minutes. Remove to a cake rack to cool. The cookies can be made a day or two ahead. Let cool and then store in an airtight container.

MAKES ABOUT 48 COOKIES

Directions for S'more Filling

1. Put a square of chocolate on each of 24 cookies.
2. Place the marshmallows on the sticks or barbecue forks.
3. Prepare a wood or charcoal fire in a fire pit or barbecue, or heat a gas grill. Hold the marshmallows over the heat, being careful not to get too close. Cook, turning, until the marshmallows are just turning golden, about 2 to 3 minutes.
4. Using a fork, push a marshmallow on top of each of the chocolate squares and top with another cookie, squeezing together to make a cookie-chocolate-marshmallow Sneetch Treat.

MAKES 24 SERVINGS

As he gobbled the cakes on his plate,
the greedy ape said as he ate,
"The greener green grapes are,
the keener keen apes are
to gobble green grape cakes.
They're GREAT!"

From *Oh Say Can You Say?*

Ape Cakes Grape Cakes

Grapes are what it takes to make these little tart-cakes, but a pudding filling and a melted-caramel topping help to create the towering shapes. For shortcuts, use ready-to-roll piecrusts and ready-to-eat pudding.

Ingredients for Tart Shells

2½ cups all-purpose flour
1 teaspoon salt
8 ounces chilled butter, cut in small pieces
½ cup ice water

Ingredients for Pudding

¼ cup cornstarch
¼ teaspoon salt
⅔ cup sugar
2 cups whole milk
1 ounce butter at room temperature
½ teaspoon vanilla
Alternatively, use 16 ounces ready-made vanilla pudding or make 2 packages instant vanilla pudding.

Ingredients for Toppings

24 caramel candy squares
1 pound seedless green grapes

Directions for Tart Shells

1. Preheat the oven to 400°F.
2. In a food processor, combine the flour and salt and mix well. Add the butter. Pulse until the mixture resembles small peas.
3. With the machine running, add the water slowly until the dough comes together, adding up to 2 more teaspoons of water if needed.
4. Divide the dough in half. Place each half on a piece of plastic wrap. Top with another piece of plastic wrap and flatten into a disk. Refrigerate overnight.
5. Leaving the plastic in place, use a rolling pin to roll each disk out to about 14 inches in diameter and ¹⁄₁₆ inch thick.
6. Using a 2-inch round biscuit or cookie cutter or the rim of a glass, cut circles

of dough. Fit the circles into muffin tins and place a little crumpled aluminum foil on top of each one. (This will keep the shells from puffing up.)

7. Bake for 5 minutes, then remove the foil and prick the bottom of each tartlet with a fork. Continue baking until golden, another 3 to 4 minutes.

8. Remove to a cake rack and let cool.

Directions for Pudding

1. In a bowl, combine the cornstarch, salt, and sugar, and stir in 1 cup of the milk to make a smooth paste.

2. In a medium saucepan, heat the remaining cup of milk over medium heat until bubbles form on the edge, about 1 minute.

3. Add the cornstarch mixture and stir constantly with a wire whisk until it boils and thickens.

4. Spoon the pudding into the top of a double boiler and place it over boiling water. Cover and cook until thickened, stirring occasionally, about 10 minutes. Remove from the heat, stir in the butter and vanilla, and pour into a bowl.

5. Let the mixture cool before filling the tarts.

May be made a day or two earlier and refrigerated.

Directions for Toppings

1. Fill each of the tart shells to the brim with the vanilla pudding.

2. Unwrap the caramel candies and place them in a shallow, microwave-safe dish. Heat in the microwave oven just long enough to melt them, about 30 to 45 seconds.

3. Drizzle caramel over the surface of the pudding. Stick grapes all over. Dip more grapes into the soft caramel and stick them to the ones in the tarts to make towers of grapes.

4. Reheat the caramel as necessary to keep it soft enough for dipping.

MAKES ABOUT 20 TO 24 TARTLETS

Every Who
Down in Who-*ville*
Liked Christmas a lot . . .
But the Grinch,
Who lived just north of Who-*ville,*
Did NOT! . . .

But,
Whatever the reason,
His heart or his shoes,
He stood there on Christmas Eve, hating the Whos,
Staring down from his cave with a sour, Grinchy frown
At the warm lighted windows below in their town.
For he knew every Who *down in* Who-*ville beneath*
Was busy now, hanging a mistletoe wreath.

From *How the Grinch Stole Christmas!*

Cindy-Lou *Who*-Wreaths

The Grinch stole all the Christmas decorations from *Who*-ville, including the wreaths. And he surely would not have been able to resist these scrumptious ones, either. You can decorate them with candy, like red hots or chocolate chips, or with nuts or dried fruit, like cherries or bananas.

Ingredients

2 teaspoons butter
16-ounce bag of marshmallows
5 cups cornflakes
½ cup dried cranberries

Directions

1. In a large saucepan over medium heat, melt the butter. Reduce the heat to low and add the marshmallows.
2. Stir until the marshmallows have melted, about 10 minutes.
3. Using a wooden spoon, stir the cornflakes into the melted marshmallows.
4. Spoon the cornflake mixture onto a sheet of wax paper and let it stand until cool enough to handle, about 10 minutes.
5. Take a large spoonful of the cornflake mixture and shape it into a wreath about 2½ inches in diameter. Place it on a clean sheet of wax paper. Repeat until all the wreaths are made.
6. Press a few dried cranberries on each of the wreaths.
7. Refrigerate until ready to serve.

MAKES ABOUT 12 WREATHS

Then he slunk to the icebox.
He took the Whos' *feast!*
He took the Who-*pudding!*
He took the roast beast!
He cleaned out that icebox as quick as a flash.
Why, that Grinch even took their last can of Who-*hash!*

From *How the Grinch Stole Christmas!*

Who-Pudding

This dessert was so delicious, the Grinch ate it every Christmas. *Who*-pudding is great any time of the year, and you can make the topping with peaches or cherries or grapes or even butterscotch chips. (But keep an eye out for the Grinch!)

Ingredients

⅓ cup plus 1 tablespoon sugar
3 tablespoons quick-cooking tapioca
2¾ cups whole milk
1 egg, well beaten
1 teaspoon vanilla
1 teaspoon finely grated orange zest
½ cup fresh or frozen raspberries
      plus 6 extra berries
¼ cup orange juice
whipped cream

Directions

1. In a medium-size saucepan, combine ⅓ cup of sugar and the tapioca, milk, and egg. Mix well, then let stand for 5 minutes.

2. Place over medium heat and bring to a full, rolling boil. Remove from the heat and stir in the vanilla and orange zest. Cool for 20 minutes, then stir. May be refrigerated and served chilled.

3. In a blender, combine ½ cup of raspberries, the orange juice, and the remaining tablespoon of sugar, then puree.

4. Pour the puree through a fine mesh strainer to remove the seeds, then drizzle the sauce in swirls over the top of the pudding.

5. Just before serving, top each bowl of pudding with a little whipped cream and a berry or two.

MAKES 4 TO 6 SERVINGS

I was real happy and carefree and young
And I lived in a place called the Valley of Vung. . . .
Now, I never had ever had
Troubles before.
So I said to myself,
"I don't want any more.
If I watch out for rocks
With my eyes straight ahead,
I'll keep out of trouble
Forever," I said.

From *I Had Trouble in Getting to Solla Sollew*

Valley of Vung's Chocolate Rocks

The Valley of Vung's chocolate rocks are trouble, all right, if you eat too many, so save some for later . . . if you can!

Ingredients

8 ounces semisweet or bittersweet chocolate
½ cup heavy cream
1 cup confectioners' sugar
½ teaspoon purple powdered food coloring or cocoa

Directions

1. Chop the chocolate into small pieces and put them in a bowl.
2. Pour the cream into a small saucepan and heat over medium heat until it bubbles around the edges.
3. Pour the hot cream over the chocolate and let it stand until the chocolate has melted, about 3 or 4 minutes. Stir until smooth.
4. Pour into a 2-inch-deep glass pie dish. Refrigerate until solid, about 3 hours.
5. Using a large melon baller or spoon, scoop out about a tablespoon of chocolate for each rock, or less for smaller rocks. Roll the chocolate between your hands to make the rock shape you want.
6. Place the chocolate rocks on a sheet of aluminum foil in a single layer.
7. Put the confectioners' sugar in a paper or plastic bag and add the purple powdered food coloring or the cocoa. Shake the bag to mix. Pour the mixture onto a plate.
8. Roll each chocolate rock in the powdered mixture and replace on the aluminum foil.
9. Refrigerate, lightly covered with aluminum foil, until you're ready to eat them.

The rocks may be refrigerated for three or four days or may be tightly covered and frozen for up to two weeks.

MAKES 20 TO 25 CHOCOLATE ROCKS, DEPENDING ON SIZE